GETTING TO KNOW THE WORLD'S GREATEST ARTISTS

GEORGIA
O'KEEFFE

WRITTEN AND ILLUSTRATED BY MIKE VENEZIA

CONSULTANT MEG MOSS

CHILDREN'S PRESS
A Division of Grolier Publishing
Sherman Turnpike
Danbury, Connecticut 06816

For my very original daughter, Elizabeth

Cover: *Cow's Skull: Red, White, and Blue.* By Georgia O'Keeffe. 1931.
Oil on canvas, 39⅞ x 35⅞ inches. The Metropolitan Museum of
Art, The Alfred Stieglitz Collection, 1952.

Library of Congress Cataloging-in-Publication Data

Venezia, Mike.
  Georgia O'Keeffe/written and illustrated by Mike
Venezia.
      p.   cm.–(Getting to know the world's greatest
artists)
  Summary: Briefly examines the life and work of the
twentieth-century artist known for her paintings of
flowers and presents examples of her art.
    ISBN 0-516-42297-9
    1.   O'Keeffe, Georgia, 1887-1986–Juvenile literature.
2.   Painters–United States–Biography–Juvenile literature.
[1.   O'Keeffe, Georgia, 1887-1986.   2.   Artists.
3.   Painting, American.   4.   Art appreciation.]
I.   Title.   II.   Series: Venezia, Mike.
Getting to know the world's greatest artists.
ND237.O5V46 1993
759.13–dc20   93-13004
[B]   CIP
                                                          AC

Georgia O'Keeffe: A Portrait, by Alfred Stieglitz. 1918.
Gelatin silver print, 3 ½ x 4 ½ inches.
National Gallery of Art, Washington, Alfred Stieglitz Collection.

Georgia O'Keeffe was born on her family's large Wisconsin farm in 1887. She would grow up to become one of America's most famous painters. Her clear, bright paintings show the beauty she found in the simple, natural things around her.

Petunia, by Georgia O'Keeffe. 1925. Oil on canvas,
18 x 22 inches. The Farber Collection, New York.

Georgia loved to paint flowers,
mountains, seashells, and even
animal bones she found in the desert.

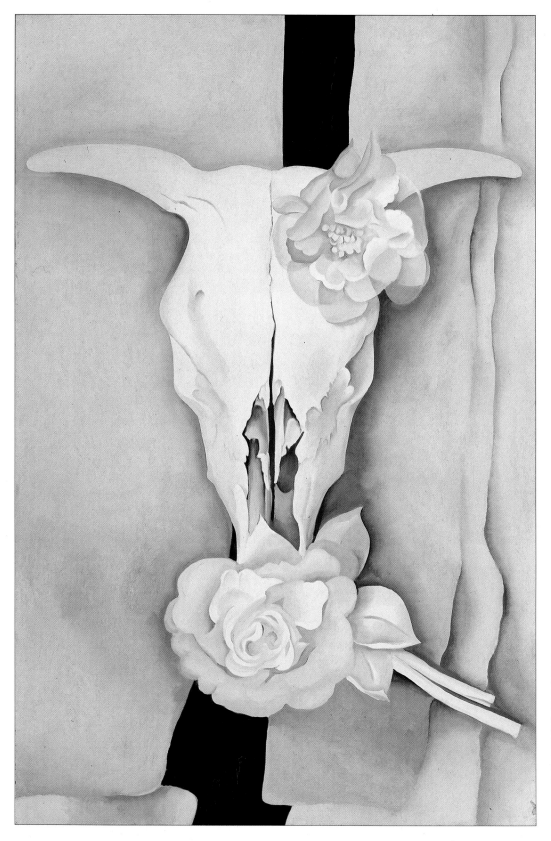

Cow's Skull with Calico Roses, by Georgia O'Keeffe. 1932. Oil on canvas, 35 9/10 x 24 inches. Gift of Georgia O'Keeffe, 1947.712. Photograph courtesy of The Art Institute of Chicago.

Sky Above Clouds IV, by Georgia O'Keeffe. 1965.
Oil on canvas, 96 x 288 inches.
Restricted gift of the Paul and Gabriella Rosenbaum Foundation,
gift of Georgia O'Keeffe, 1983.821.
Photograph © 1993, The Art Institute of Chicago.
All Rights Reserved.

Even though Georgia was interested in all kinds of natural

things, she hardly ever painted
pictures of people or animals.

White Shell with Red, by Georgia O'Keeffe. 1938. Pastel on paper, 21 x 27 inches.
Alfred Stieglitz Collection, bequest of Georgia O'Keeffe, 1987.250.5.
Photograph courtesy of The Art Institute of Chicago.

Georgia often rearranged the
natural things she saw, and simplified
them. She made the seashell above
very large, to give it a special power
and strength.

Blue and Green Music, by Georgia O'Keeffe. 1919. Oil on canvas, 23 x 19 inches.
Alfred Stieglitz Collection, gift of Georgia O'Keeffe, 1969.835.
Photograph © 1992, The Art Institute of Chicago. All Rights Reserved.

Sometimes she painted shapes
and colors that she saw in her mind.

The farm where Georgia grew up was a great place to learn about nature. Georgia wanted to touch and feel everything she could get her hands on.

Georgia remembered that when she was very little, she put dirt in her mouth to see what it tasted like!

Georgia's mother thought art was very important, and made sure Georgia and her sisters had art lessons while they were growing up. Georgia did so well with her lessons that her parents encouraged her to go to art college after she graduated from high school. Georgia studied at different art schools and colleges all over the country.

Dead Rabbit with Copper Pot, by Georgia O'Keeffe. 1908.
Oil on canvas, 19 x 23½ inches.
Art Students League, New York. Photograph by Dave Forbert.

At one school, in New York City,
she won a prize for her painting of
a rabbit and copper pot.

Georgia liked New York City. It was busier and more exciting than the peaceful farm areas where she had grown up. Georgia often visited a small gallery in New York that showed the work of new artists. It was owned by a well-known photographer named Alfred Stieglitz.

Alfred loved modern art and tried to get people interested in modern European artists, like Paul Cezanne

Above: *The Large Bathers*, by Paul Cezanne. 1906. Oil on canvas, 82 x 99 inches. Philadelphia Museum of Art, purchased, W.P. Wilstach Collection.

Below: *The Red Studio,* by Henri Matisse. 1911. Oil on canvas, 71¼ x 86¼ inches. The Museum of Modern Art, New York, Mrs. Simon Guggenheim Fund. Photograph © 1993, The Museum of Modern Art, New York.

and Henri Matisse, and American artists, like John Marin and Marsden Hartley.

Georgia didn't know it at the time, but in a few years, Alfred would help get people interested in her paintings, too.

Above: *Painting No. 48,* by Marsden Hartley. 1913. Oil on canvas, 47³⁄₁₆ x 47³⁄₁₆ inches. The Brooklyn Museum, Dick S. Ramsay Fund.

After finishing school, Georgia decided to teach art for a while, and traveled to Texas to take a job there. She found it an exciting place to be. Georgia loved the clear skies and the hot, bright sun. She felt the energy and power of the dust storms and heat lightning she saw at night.

Evening Star, No. V, by Georgia O'Keeffe. 1917.
Watercolor, 8 ⅝ x 11 ⅝ inches. Marion Koogler McNay Art Museum,
San Antonio, Texas, Bequest of Helen Miller Jones.

Georgia started to show the excitement she felt about Texas in her paintings. Soon her work looked different from the work of any other artist.

During this time, Alfred Stieglitz became very interested in Georgia

O'Keeffe. He remembered her from her visits to his gallery, and had seen some of her newest works of art. Alfred thought Georgia could become one of the best American artists ever.

Alfred wrote a letter to Georgia and asked her to come back to New York. He told her he could raise enough money so she wouldn't have to work and could spend all her time painting. He also offered to show her artwork in his gallery.

Georgia found it hard to leave the beauty of Texas, but decided Alfred's offer was too good to miss out on.

After she arrived in New York, Georgia began painting bold shapes

Red Canna, by
Georgia O'Keeffe.
c. 1923.
Oil on canvas,
36 x 29 ⅞ inches.
Collection of
The University of
Arizona Museum,
Tucson, Gift of
Oliver James.

and designs, covering her canvases
with bright color. Soon her work
changed, and she began painting the
beautiful flowers that helped to make
her famous.

Morning Glory with Black, by Georgia O'Keeffe. c. 1926. Oil on canvas, 35 13/16 x 39 5/8 inches. The Cleveland Museum of Art, Bequest of Leonard C. Hanna, Jr., 58.42.

Georgia usually made her flowers very large. She hoped they would make people feel the same wonderful way she felt when she looked at real flowers. Georgia thought her large

flowers might even get busy New
Yorkers to stop and notice them.

Georgia's paintings got attention
right away. At first, people were
curious to see the work of a woman
artist. In the 1920s, there weren't
many well-known women artists. It
didn't take long for people to realize
that Georgia O'Keeffe wasn't just a
woman artist. She was a great
American artist!

Even though Georgia needed
money to live, she felt funny about
selling her art. Georgia worked hard
on her paintings, and felt so close to
them that she hated to see them leave
the gallery. They were almost like her
children.

Georgia O'Keeffe: A Portrait—Head, by Alfred Stieglitz. 1918.
Palladium print, toned with gold, 9½ x 7⅝ inches.
National Gallery of Art, Washington, Alfred Stieglitz Collection.

In between painting and showing her work, Georgia agreed to model for Alfred Stieglitz. Alfred thought Georgia was very beautiful and took many famous photographs of her.

East River from the 30th Story of the Shelton Hotel,
by Georgia O'Keeffe. 1928. Oil on canvas, 30 x 48 inches.
From the collection of the New Britain Museum of American Art,
Connecticut, Stephen Lawrence Fund. Photograph by E. Irving Blomstrann.

Alfred and Georgia had respected
each other's talent for a long time.
Now that Georgia was living in
New York and working closely with
Alfred, they found themselves falling
in love. In 1924, they decided to get
married.

They moved into an apartment high up in a big hotel. Georgia loved the wide-open view she saw, and started painting pictures of the city. This surprised people, because in the 1920s, powerful city scenes were usually done only by men.

New York, Night, by Georgia O'Keeffe.
1928-29. Oil on canvas,
40⅛ x 19⅛ inches.
Sheldon Memorial Art Gallery,
University of Nebraska-Lincoln,
Nebraska Art Association-
Thomas C. Woods Memorial Collection.

Grey Hills, by Georgia O'Keeffe. 1942.
Oil on canvas, 20 x 30 inches. © 1993 Indianapolis Museum of Art,
Gift of Mr. and Mrs. James W. Fesler.

Several years later, Georgia was invited out West to visit some friends in New Mexico. She thought the desert and clear blue skies there were even more exciting than the scenery in Texas. Georgia began painting the animal bones, desert flowers, and sun-baked adobe churches she found there.

Georgia especially loved the mountains in New Mexico. They seemed almost alive to her. In some paintings, you might get the feeling that Georgia's mountains could get up and move around.

Ranchos Church, by Georgia O'Keeffe.
c. 1930. Oil on canvas, 24 x 36 inches.
The Phillips Collection, Washington, D.C.

Georgia spent most of the rest
of her life painting in New Mexico.
Alfred agreed it was the best place
for her to be in order to make her
paintings as good as possible.

Georgia only traveled back to New York for a few months every year to be with Alfred and show her work. Years later, after Alfred died, Georgia moved to New Mexico for good.

Georgia O'Keeffe lived to be 98 years old. She decided to become an artist at a time when it was proper only for women to teach art.

Photo by Philippe Halsman. 1948.
Kodachrome, 4 x 5 inches.
© by Yvonne Halsman.

Georgia didn't care what people thought about her, or her art. She worked hard on her paintings and put her own special feeling into them.

Black Cross, New Mexico, by Georgia O'Keeffe. 1929.
Oil on canvas, 39 x 30 inches.
Art Institute Purchase Fund, 1943.95.
Photograph courtesy of The Art Institute of Chicago.

Georgia met many famous artists during her life. She learned a lot from them, but never copied their styles or joined their groups.

Pelvis with the Distance, by Georgia O'Keeffe. 1943.
Oil on canvas, 23⅞ x 29¾ inches.
© Indianapolis Museum of Art, Gift of Anne Marmon Greenleaf in memory of Carolyn Marmon Fesler.

Pattern of Leaves, by Georgia O'Keeffe. 1924.
Oil on canvas, 22⅛ x 18⅛ inches.
The Phillips Collection, Washington, D.C.

Because of this, Georgia O'Keeffe's paintings are very original. She often found beauty in things that most people would ignore or never even notice, and was able to show that beauty in her paintings.

If you get a chance to see a real Georgia O'Keeffe painting, you'll probably notice how bright and clear the colors are. This is because Georgia paid special attention to her painting materials. She always bought the best brushes and paint, no matter how much they cost her.

The paintings in this book come from the museums listed below.